The Collection 2015

An Hachette UK Company
www.hachette.co.uk

First published in Great Britain in 2014 by Hamlyn,
a division of Octopus Publishing Group Ltd, Endeavour House, 189 Shaftesbury Avenue,
London, WC2H 8JY

www.octopusbooks.co.uk

Giles ® is a registered trademark of Express Newspapers
Text and images copyright © Express Newspapers 2014
Design layout copyright © Octopus Publishing Group Ltd 2014
Foreword copyright © Pattemore Entertainment LLP 2014
Photograph of Lynda Bellingham © Alan Olley 2014

Cartoons supplied by British Cartoon Archive
Cartoons compiled by John Field

ISBN 978 0 60062 457 8

A CIP catalogue record for this book is available from the British Library.

Printed and bound in China

10 9 8 7 6 5 4 3 2 1

The Collection 2015

compiled by John Field
foreword by Lynda Bellingham

EXPRESS NEWSPAPERS

hamlyn

Contents

Foreword

Lynda Bellingham

Picking up a collection of Giles cartoons is akin to leafing through the family album. Fifty years of goings on in all our lives. It is really quite remarkable how the drawings are so familiar once again. I grew up with Giles cartoons in my consciousness from an early age. My father loved them and would sit at the breakfast table chuckling to himself. In the early days I was too young to understand the humour but I loved examining the drawings and seeing all the different characters. Seeing some of the cartoons now makes me think of the *Where's Wally* pictures I enjoyed with my boys when they were young. There is no actual Wally in a Giles cartoon but there are so many wonderful characters and so many incidents taking place in various corners of a drawing, it is just as challenging to the eye as trying to find Wally!

My dad was a pilot with the British Overseas Airways Corporation for years, and then a farmer for the rest of his life, so he could identify with the characters and humour that Giles inspired. Looking at the collection of works now, it is extraordinary how little has really changed in our society. Attitudes to the countryside have always been tinged with the idea that somehow urban life is gritty and on the edge, while the countryside is full of toffs and idiots. This ridiculous misconception used to really annoy my dad, as it does me. But with a few astute drawings from Giles that myth is dispelled. The cartoons are full of angry farmers and crafty poachers. Complaints about food prices and wages have never changed and neither has nature. There is even

a cartoon, dated 1947, of farmers swimming across their flooded fields! One thing that struck me looking at some of the drawings of the countryside was the beauty and accuracy of Giles's talent – it was not just about his humour or comment on society and happenings around him. The atmosphere he engendered of winter, in the cartoons of a farmer ploughing a field was tangible. I could feel the icy wind bending the leafless trees, and remember the hard clods of ploughed earth frozen in furrows. It was a hard landscape and a hard life captured so poetically by the cartoonist's pen and ink.

The historical value of Giles cartoons is enormous. There are so many reminders of moments of real importance in our social history. It is a fantastic way to remind oneself of the last fifty years. Perhaps the collections should be part of the school curriculum? What a lovely way to learn history. March 25th 1980 he says in a cartoon: "Once it was 'You've never had it so good', now it's: 'You've had it worse', tomorrow it'll probably be: 'You've had it!'"

I reserve my final words on the subject of how much I love Giles for Grandma. All I can say is, respect! If ever they made a film of the family I would be first in line to play the great lady. She is a legend in her own cartoons and worthy of an Oscar for best newcomer, aged eighty!

Giles's Britain – Introduction

During his long cartoon-drawing career, which covered almost the whole second half of the last century, Carl Giles touched upon just about every aspect of life in our country. Through his cartoons he commented, in his own unique way, upon the many ups and downs of life in Britain during that period, including the austerity period following World War Two, political intrigues, economic booms and busts, sporting successes and failures, scandals, strikes and much else of national importance. He also touched upon more ordinary things like the weather, his battles with such personal irritants as a line of electricity pylons being erected across his Suffolk farm and a long-standing feud with local traffic wardens outside his studio-office in Ipswich as well as his deeply-felt dislike of the more pompous and self-important individuals in our society.

With such a broad body of work, it is not surprising that he also produced a fairly wide pictorial record of Britain. In this year's collection, therefore, I have concentrated upon those cartoons which provide a sort of illustrated guide book of our country, with England divided into basic regions and Scotland and Wales having their own chapters.

We start, however, with a chapter covering a number of cartoons from Giles's journeys around Britain with his wife, Joan. Quite early on after the War, Giles decided to build his own caravan to use on holidays, designed to double up as a mobile studio. Giles designed his caravan with a special part of a wall which could be projected out to provide a very convenient drawing board facility whilst at rest on tour. Whether this requirement impinged seriously upon the comfort of the interior layout of the caravan is not known as there is no record, so far as I can ascertain, of Joan complaining. This mobile facility did, however, allow Giles to continue to provide Express Newspapers with a full supply of cartoons, even when away from his studio.

As illustrated in this first chapter, Giles made good use of various experiences during these caravanning excursions in some of his cartoons. They provide a useful record of some of his travels around the country and it is to be regretted that he and Joan did not make more of these journeys so that we would be able to enjoy a larger number of cartoons from other parts of the country not fully covered in his work. Although, in his vast workload, there is a wide selection of cartoons using London locations, only a relatively small number are included here as good coverage of these already appears in *Giles's London*.

Not surprisingly, I have been able to identify a large number of Giles's cartoons based on Ipswich and the surrounding areas of Suffolk, where he lived and worked for almost his whole career. No doubt, it was often convenient for him to use a scene from the local area as a basis for a cartoon. I also believe however, that sometimes, when he was late in producing a cartoon and the time was approaching for the last train to London (which took the finished work up to Liverpool Street to be collected and rushed to Fleet Street by taxi) he would have to find a nearby location, in the streets around his studio, as a basis for the cartoon in order to meet the deadline. I have included, however, only a small number of these locally-based cartoons in this collection.

It is difficult, when describing any collection of Giles's work, to overstate the importance of his make-believe family in the world which, as a cartoonist, he created. He frequently used the family as a vehicle for illustrating events, both of national or lesser importance, and of course, Grandma often took centre stage, even when away from home. A small number of cartoons containing the family, included in this collection, are based in Blackpool and, as a result, we have two national icons together – the Tower and Grandma (I am not sure which is the more indestructible!). It was on one of the trips up north, that we find, in cartoon dated August 21, 1957 (included), that she has a sister in Manchester. However, in a cartoon dated December 2, 1963 (included), it turns out that, in fact, there are two sisters up north. And then, to make matters worse, in a cartoon dated June 25, 1974 (not included in this collection as it simply shows Grandma, at home, playing the bagpipes – celebrating Scotland's qualification for the 1974 World Cup Finals), we discover that she has yet another 'wee sister' in Aberdeen. Further research, see cartoon dated May 6, 1984 (included), reveals that there is also another sister living somewhere between Aberystwyth and Lampeter. Unfortunately, I cannot be sure that that is all!

There is no doubt that Giles, with his obvious love of Britain's wide range of regional traditions and folklore, enjoyed including local themes and oddities in his cartoons – the

railway station in Wales with the impossibly long name, Nessie, the Pirates of Penzance, the Highland Games, the Lancashire-Yorkshire divide, Lady Godiva and many others all appear. His work also includes a number of our country's greatest buildings, including castles, cathedrals and stately homes. I suspect that sometimes he copied certain locations from photographs but I am sure that, at other times, he drew from life, particularly those cartoons which appeared during the periods when he was on tour, with his caravan, in different parts of the country.

Throughout his work, Giles's drawing style varied considerably from cartoon to cartoon with some very detailed, almost architectural, drawings (see cartoon dated November 27, 1963 of Manchester Central Library and Town Hall) whilst others, such as cartoon dated June 5, 1951 of Hull docks (included), simply give an impression. In some cases, his drawings provide a fairly detailed historical record of a building which has since disappeared or been fundamentally changed. An example of this is the cartoon, dated May 8, 1951 (included), of the Shakespeare Memorial Theatre in Stratford-Upon-Avon, which has been re-modelled and extended in recent years.

I hope that this collection will fully display not only Giles's unique sense of humour and accomplished drawing skills, but also his ability to capture on paper some of our most iconic and historic places as well as many of the idiosyncratic features and themes, which are an important part of the diverse and fascinating character of our country.

John Field

Giles on tour

The Yak was a Soviet World War Two fighter being used by the North Korean forces in the Korean War, which had started just over two months before this cartoon appeared.

"So far, all your quiet-little-caravan-holiday-away-from-it-all hasn't got is Yaks and North Koreans."

Suffolk

Daily Express, September 8, 1950

LRT 140 was the registration number of Giles's long-suffering Land Rover which he always used for towing the caravan.

"That was a fine idea back at head office telling them to look out for LRT 140 in yesterday's Express..."

Daily Express, May 9, 1951

Stratford-upon-Avon

Maybe this actually happened.

"Well, now, if it isn't Gipsy Giles, all nicely camped in a no-parking area."

"I've chased you all over the Midlands with this, but I'm 'anged if I'm going to chase you all over the Lake District."

14   Following the Second World War, the Class Z Reserve Contingent of the British Forces was formed consisting of demobbed servicemen. Giles may have had a drink or two in the Officers' Mess the evening before.

"Just a moment, Sir! During the course of a drink or so in the Officers' Mess, I understand you signed on for four years military service."

"Now I'm not going to worry you for a £525 bonus like they get in the R.A.F. – I'd simply like a pair of trousers that fit."

"Goodbye, Colonel – many thanks for letting me park my studio-caravan on your gunsite."

Rush the family dog arriving home at Giles's farm after the trip up north.

"Stand by for some lengthy reminiscing on 'Now-when-I-was-in-Manchester...'"

The Giles family left this morning (weather permitting or not) by caravan for its holiday.

Leaving home

Daily Express, August 14, 1951

"Dad's getting on well with the neighbours, Mum."

"Caravan? The caravan came off hours ago."

Arriving home

Daily Express, September 11, 1951

It has been recorded that Giles enjoyed being with circus folk.

THE GILES FAMILY, circus-bound, in their studio-caravan, have been fog-bound, ice-bound, but have at last reached the circus winter quarters at Ascot where they will be living for a while. Nevertheless, there will be a slight delay with funny jokes about circuses while a certain amount of thawing-out takes place.

Daily Express, December 9, 1952

Ascot

No caption appeared with this cartoon – we can only guess at Father's thoughts.

Scotland

Daily Express, August 31, 1954

"Look out, Dad! Here comes the man to say no more Highland Games rehearsals."

Scotland

"What have we stopped to celebrate this time – the Battle of Bannockburn or Battle of Britain Week?"

Inverness

Daily Express, September 15, 1954

dear all,

plodding north through rain hail hurrycanes and fog to find out what mr ailsham oggs doing about bringing prosperity to the north we found a little hole in the clouds clear enough to show us we were miles off the main road on top of a darbyshire hill

my picture shoes: 1. mr giles telling george he don't think george is a very nice navigator. 2. mrs giles saying she's had all she wants of ailsham oggs bells. 3. auntie vera wimpring because there isn't a kemist in sight. 4. auntie vera's baby wimpring 5. grandma stretching her legs and saying she don't think much of the mod. con. 6. larry souvineer hunting. 7. the dogs just been told we don't want a lot of noise. 8. vulchers. more next week i'm afraid.

yours truly, giles junior.

Daily Express, November 23, 1963   *Derbyshire*

"We are going to need Mr. Ailsham 'Ogg's better roads if your little lad's going to keep losing his ball during rush hours."

Mersey Tunnel

Daily Express, November 28, 1963

At this time, Parliament was discussing the culling of a large number of grey seals on the Farne Islands.

"Our Vera thought she heard a baby seal calling for help."

London

This cartoon is probably linked to a heated Government debate at the time concerning the banning of communist and fascist employees from security Departments such as the War Office. The white conical hats and robes are reminiscent of those worn at some Spanish Holy Week processions (normally falling at this time of the year) and traditionally linked with such things as routing out heretics.

Whitehall

Sunday Express, March 21, 1948

Two days earlier the Government had announced that police on duty in Downing Street would be armed as a security precaution.
At the time there was strong feeling about the "Ireland Bill" being discussed, which was concerned with the relationship of the UK with Ireland.

"That's what comes of arming the Downing Street Police – little holes in our hats."

Sunday Express, May 15, 1949

Houses of Parliament

The Queen's Welsh corgi, Susan, has bitten a Grenadier Guardsman in the ankle. Now while there is apparently no penalty for corgis who bite Guardsmen, the punishment for Guardsmen who say "Ouch" on duty is pretty stiff. So the Guardsman stood his ground as if nobody had bitten him at all. News of this fascinating little game of Susan's quickly spread to the rest of the doggie world.

Buckingham Palace

Daily Express, July 1, 1954

The day before, the BBC had arranged for the Trooping of the Colour ceremony to be broadcast live to the Russians on Moscow TV Central Network.

"Technically speaking, Farquharson, to the TV viewers in Moscow we're just another 'Western'."

Sunday Express, June 11, 1961

Horse Guards

"Another Communist-inspired wildcat strike."

Tower of London

Alfred George "Alfie" Hinds was a British criminal who, while serving a 12-year prison sentence for robbery, successfully broke out of three high security prisons.

"You'd be a little happy if you were a warder who's had to keep an eye on Aflie Hinds."

Sunday Express, August 2, 1964

HMP Pentonville

Halfway through his first tenure as British Prime Minister, Harold Wilson brought his yellow labrador puppy to Downing Street.

"This sort of thing isn't going to help my public image, Paddy me boy."

"Not quite in the language of the Immortal Bard, but the gentleman says he fears this is the wrong barge."

Regent's Canal

This was the time of the Apollo 11 mission to the moon which brought back samples of lunar rocks.

"On the other hand, have you got any proof they're NOT genuine?"

BT Tower

Daily Express, July 15, 1969

"Your wife's downstairs, Sir – she's decided to keep you company on the train to your four-day conference in the Midlands."

The Admiralty

East of England

During the war and post-war period, the word "spiv" was used for petty criminals dealing in dodgy goods. One source states that the word was originally racecourse slang, hence, presumably, the connection made by Giles, whose grandfather was a racehorse jockey at Newmarket.

"I see they've got the Spivs out again."

The Oaksey Report contained recommendations for improved scales of pay in addition to recommendations relating to pensions for the police forces. For over 20 years, Giles had his studio in this street, the Buttermarket, and, throughout that period, had an ongoing battle with the police, and later the traffic wardens, regarding his inclination to park his car exactly where this gentleman has left his.

"Quick! Go over and be nice to them. Tell them you think the Oaksey Plan is wonderful."

"This type of craft, sir, is very simple to handle – from the look of things it need be."

Norfolk Broads

In July 1951, Randolph Turpin won the world middleweight title by beating the then champion, Sugar Ray Robinson, in London. However, in New York on 12 September, Robinson won the crown back with a tenth-round technical knockout. At that time many thousands of US servicemen were stationed in the Woodbridge area.

"Lay off, honey – ain't my fault an American beat Turpin."

The quote is from John Masefield's poem "Sea-Fever". The pub is the Maybush in Waldringfield – a pub well-known to Giles as he kept his boat there and, over the years, gave the local sailing club many original sailing-themed cartoons. A copy of this cartoon appears in the pub.

"I must go down to the sea again, to the lonely sea and the sky..."

Waldringfield

Sunday Express, July 20, 1952

I cannot be sure that this is the same Welsh sister that Grandma was visiting in cartoon dated 6 May 1984 – maybe this is yet another one!

41

"Grandma, one more gloomy weather forecast because your corns hurt and you won't GET a lift to your sister Fanny in Llanfihangel-Glyn-Myfyr."

Daily Express, November 12, 1952

Norwich Castle

"They're wearing smog masks so that their navigators can't hear what they're calling them."

Norwich Cathedral

Daily Express, November 11, 1953

"Despite the fact that Grandma's corns were giving her what-ho this morning there will be brilliant sunshine everywhere."
(Meteorological report)

Daily Express, June 10, 1954

Oulton Broad

This is Westerfield Station, just north of Ipswich. Giles passed by on his way into town from his farm – his Land Rover LRT 140 appears parked in the background.

"Christmas holidays are not what they used to be, Millie – seven days discussing nuclear fission instead of ailments."

Westerfield Station

Sunday Express, January 5, 1955

The previous day, the Home Secretary announced that he proposed to appoint an independent body to "examine, with authority and impartiality, the relationship of the police with the general public".

"Madam would go a long way towards improving her public relationship with the police if she would kindly remove her car from my foot."

The strike was over the sacking of a shop steward and lasted several weeks.

"There was my mum holding forth at this workers' wives rally when in came a bunch of directors' wives –
Boy! Talk about a punch-up."

Dagenham

Daily Express, November 15, 1962

The day before, US President Kennedy suggested a joint Soviet-American expedition to the moon, saying that such co-operation "could stem from the reduction in tension now possible between East and West in the wake of the Nuclear Test Ban Treaty".

"Here's one mixed crew that hasn't got a language problem, Georgie."

This is part of Giles's campaign against the Central Electricity Generating Board relating to a line of large pylons which it constructed crossing his land, spoiling his view of open countryside.

"I hope this client knows what he's doing – giving us a bob for every pylon we knock down on his farm."

Giles's farm

Sunday Express, April 18, 1965

Students at Cambridge tried to overturn the car taking Mr. Denis Healey, Minister of Defence, back to London after a lecture. There was general unhappiness among students, throughout the country, over grants.

"To take action against the students who mobbed Mr. Healey would not be desirable or practicable." (The Rev. Donald Cupitt, Senior Proctor at Cambridge)

Prince Charles, about halfway through his course at Trinity College, Cambridge, had just started flying lessons and had made his first solo flight, at RAF Bassingbourn, on January 14, 1969. In addition, although he was created Prince of Wales on July 26, 1958, his actual investiture as such was to be conducted at Caernarfon Castle later that year (July 1).

"Ask his Royal Highness to come to my office when he's finished his solo flight."

Two days earlier, nine Hells Angels appeared in court following disturbances at a pop festival in Weeley, Essex. Their punishment varied greatly from 12 months' imprisonment for maliciously wounding someone, to a £15 fine for possessing a truncheon. She seems a little annoyed that he had not been more violent.

"Honestly, Chick – it wan't my fault they only fined me one pound and the rest of the boys got six months."

Daily Express, September 2, 1971

Colchester

52 In response to an increase in car theft, the police were recommending the introduction of car security systems into car design and the installation of devices that disabled the vehicle when parked.

"Don't congratulate me on taking all reasonable precautions to immobilise my car – they've nicked my wheels."

Ipswich

Daily Express, September 30, 1971

Nicole, Duchess of Bedford, was the third wife of Ian, 13th Duke of Bedford. By 1974, Woburn Abbey had become the most popular stately home in the country when the Duke and Duchess departed suddenly to live in France. In that same year the Duchess had created a sensation when she wrote in her memoirs about a bizarre incident in which she had been held captive in a Manchester hotel room for three days by a stranger.

"And don't you keep a-looking at me, yer varmint."

"Funny, it looked much bigger at the Boat Show."

Pin Mill

"Go forth and speed the gospel to our flocks and at all times keep your eye on the Fuzz."

Sunday Express, May 11, 1975

Norwich Cathedral

"She says we made Dunkirk in 1940, so we can make it again to pick up her sister, Florrie."

Felixstowe Ferry

Daily Express, August 19, 1980

For the first time in the history of the Boat Race one team, Oxford, decided to use a female cox.

"Anything they can do we can do better!"

Cambridge

"It's not all bad having a US Base next door – Uncle Jim and the Aunts have decided on Cornwall this year instead of staying with us."

Suffolk

"Listen, Elmer, we've got Bob Hope tomorrow, Danny Kaye Thursday – but it's going to be Bill Shake and Henry Four tonight.
Now stop beefing."

Daily Express, May 8, 1951

Stratford-upon-Avon

Lady Godiva, was an 11th-century noblewoman who rode naked through the streets of Coventry to protest against the taxation imposed by her husband on his tenants.

"You'll get 'It's-quite-all-right-we-learned-all-about-her-at-school' if you're not all down here in ten seconds."

King George VI opened the Festival of Britain in London on May 3, 1951. It promoted Britain's contributions to science, technology and the arts and attracted large crowds.

"Have a nice day oop t'Festival yesterday, Mac?"

"Miners get everything these days, pit-head baths, race horses for pit ponies, bulletins on Rita Hayworth down at coal-face..."

Stoke-on-Trent

"There goes one of your 'Holier than thou' brigade. Husband's on night shift at Jaguars."

"It says here, Vera, that story about live alligators in the canal has been denied."

Leicester

"I don't know who put the idea in her head – but she says she won't appear till the Royalty get here."

That week, Mick Jagger's girlfriend, Marianne Faithfull, played her first night as Irina in Chekov's *The Three Sisters* at the Royal Court theatre in London.

"'Tis but a teenage jest, thou sayest? By the Bard, it had better be, says I."

Stratford-upon-Avon

Daily Express, April 18, 1967

At this time, the US was experiencing unemployment and inflation rate problems and, following a secret meeting at Camp David two days earlier, President Nixon had issued a series of economic measures, which became known as the "Nixon Shock".

"Nixon's US-on-the-rocks speech sure helped our overseas economy. Honey, that's the third guide who's tipped me this morning."

Daily Express, August 17, 1971

Stratford-upon-Avon

The new Ford Sierra, replacing the Ford Cortina, was first unveiled on September 22, 1982 and sales commenced one week before this cartoon appeared. Its aerodynamic styling was considered ahead of its time and, as such, was the subject of some debate.

"I'm suddenly developing a total allergy to your mother running on about the wonderful new Ford Sierra."

Birmingham

Daily Express, October 21, 1982

Felix, a cat, had travelled the world for 29 days in the cargo hold of a plane, having escaped his cage. It was estimated that he had spend 377 hours in the air and visited 19 cities. He was flown back home VIP-style. Nothing is known about the fish's travels.

"Great disparity in fare charges – 12p for a fish to go by bus yet a cat can fly round the world for free with VIP treatment."

The North

The man was referring to the Skylon, a vertical metal structure at the Festival of Britain, which caused some concerns about danger to visitors from lightning strikes.

"Blackpool's got everything t'Festival's got, lad – except one o'those things where you get all struck by lightning if you're underneath."

Blackpool

Daily Express, May 24, 1951

"Your Dome of Discovery's seen nothing 'til it's seen a coachload of us girls in London for the day." (Haworth Cotton Mill, Salford)

Daily Express, May 29, 1951

Salford

In 1951, part of Battersea Park, including a boating lake, was transformed into a Pleasure Garden as part of the Festival of Britain.

"Then after tea we could spend the evening in one of those little boats on Battersea Lake...."

Hull

Daily Express, June 5, 1951

"Good afternoon gentlemen. We shall be paying particular attention to the little old expense returns up to and INCLUDING April the fifth."

Daily Express, April 6, 1952

Aintree

"...You and your 'Let's sit under that hedge out of the wind.'"

"My dad reckons that anyone who has to spend all day with us ought to get the same as a Hollywood film star."

Grandma Giles arrived in the North to begin a holiday with her younger sister Millie. Both of them were in a bit of a huff due to the fact that Grandma Giles nearly always is and Grandma Millie had been waiting in the rain for several hours. 'Twas an unfortunate coincidence that this first illustration had to be a wet one, but Northerners must not think I am carrying on the old worn joke about Manchester and its rain. It was raining in the South when Grandma G left, it was raining all the way across to the West where she discovered she was on the wrong coach, it rained all the way back to the South, and it rained all the way up to the North. If it keeps raining all the time she's there it won't matter much as neither of the Grandmas is what you call the outdoor type. The remark by the driver unloading Grandma G's fifth heavy suitcase: "What have you got in this one, luv – sun tan oil?" was ignored. And rain or no rain, the fine fresh breezes from the Manchester Canal were more than welcomed by the passengers who had spent the journey trapped in an aroma of peppermints, liniments, and camphor balls. More tomorrow, I fear.

Manchester

Daily Express, August 20, 1957

"No fear! We'll toss for it. I served them when they were here last year."

One of the reasons Grandma Giles took to the North for a holiday with her younger sister was because she wanted to be alone with the peace and quiet of the Blackpool sand and saloons–away from anybody who kept a check on her frequent desires to let rip. So when the Lancashire police decided to use Blackpool and district to try out their new radar and speed traps and booked Grandma and sister Millie for belting up and down the Central Beach she took it as a personal affront, claiming that her local copper back home put 'em up to it. When the sergeant said: "What's trying to do, lass–bust sound barrier?" Grandma's reply was the first shot fired during her holiday likely to stew-up Northern-Southern relations for a long time.

Blackpool

Daily Express, August 22, 1957

Concluding this pictorial record of Grandma Giles's holiday does not mean that she's had enough of Blackpool but that I've had enough of Grandma and her sister Millie for one week. And what better place to wind up a holiday in than one of those quiet, restful hostels so popular in the North.

The index might help. 1. Grandma's sister explaining that if it wasn't for the bad weather and shortage of money these days the place would be packed. 2. Visitor telling Native that Blackpool's a fine place and he's coming again next year. 3. His wife thinking not if she knows it. 4. Visitor saying this Blackpool air suits him. 5. Native saying Aye, he can see that. 6. Visitor singing "Rock Me Baby." 7. Native from Burtonwood explaining about the American who went up 19 miles in a balloon this week. 8. Lady friend asking why Native from Burtonwood can't take her up in a balloon. 9. Another Native from Burtonwood saying "I guess you're high enough already, Honey." 10. Gentleman escort of No. 11 wishing everyone from Burtonwood was 19 miles up in a balloon. 11. See 10. 12. Someone singing "Galway Bay." 13. Someone singing "Will Ye No Come Back Again?" 14. Native asking piano man: "Do you know your – row is breaking my – eardrums?" 15. Piano man replying "No–but if you've got the music I'll play it." (Old joke, new version). 16. Someone singing he's a lassie from Lancashire. 17. Visitor telling barman he gave him a quid and only got change for ten bob. 18. Barman saying [sic]. 19. Someone singing he does like to be beside the seaside. The rest is fairly straight-forward.

Daily Express, August 24, 1957

Blackpool

On December 5, 1958, the first British motorway was opened around Preston. It was just over eight miles in length and was the beginning of a new era of motoring in Britain. Some people at the time thought, however, that such a road, designed for high speeds, would be very dangerous and anticipated a spate of accidents.

"Well, so long, Harry – you'll find our insurance in the little tin box in the cupboard under the stairs."

By November 1963, the Beatles had become the biggest band in Britain and a few days before this cartoon appeared, they played in Manchester. By this time, their hairstyles had also become famous, particularly that of Paul McCartney whose hair flopped over his eyes as he sang. Stinker's hair style did, in fact, pre-date the Beatles.

"I said you were asking for it, trying to sue the Beatles for pinching your hair style."

Daily Express, November 27, 1963

Manchester

"Vera's done it again – let someone sell her Manchester racecourse in exchange for her green stamps and Post Office savings."

Manchester

Daily Express, November 29, 1963

The Jodrell Bank Observatory was established in 1945 by Sir Bernard Lovell, a radio astronomer at the University of Manchester, and used for space research including the tracking of space probes.

"Never mind about it being 'only your Grandma in there sleeping it off after celebrating Sir Winston's birthday' – her snores are playing old harry at Jodrell Bank."

Sunday Express, December 1, 1963

Cheshire

"Stand by for a fab bout of Blackpool hospitality, daddyo – here come two of Grandma's northern sisters."

Blackpool

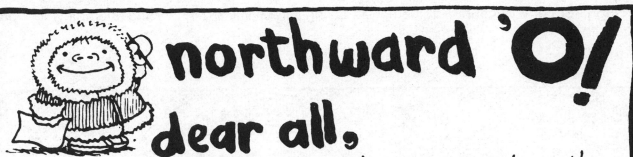

northward 'O!

dear all,

pressing hon with our tour of the north we've just done a sort of figure 8 round oldham, uddersfeild, doosbry, wakefeild, leeds, halfax, littelborrow, todmordon, hebden bridge, (i like hedden bridge,) bradford and burnly.

it wasn't meant be a figure 8 but what with evrybody driving and the fog that's way it turned out. i enclose a few snaps of the family on root,

yours truly, giles junior

granma mumbling why can't she stay in blackpool with her sisters (i call them aunty granmas)

aunty vera sneezing in uddersfeild. (vera's sneez has a diffrent note for evry town in the north)

Politician Quintin Hogg, formerly Viscount Hailsham, was taking a keen interest in tackling unemployment problems in the north.

"If your 'Ailsham 'Ogg's so concerned about the North, what's he doing about United?"

The previous March, Labour had won the election and Edward Heath took over the leadership of the Conservative Party. James Callaghan was the Chancellor of the Exchequer at this time.

"I told you that bounder who asked if we'd like a ride and left us stuck up here looked a bit like Jim Callaghan."

Daily Express, October 13, 1966

Blackpool

The annual Labour Party Conference was being held at Scarborough. Barbara Castle was the Minister of Transport at the time and was introducing the Road Safety Act 1967, which made it an offence to drive a motor vehicle with a blood alcohol concentration exceeding a prescribed legal limit.

"60% Pepsicola, 25% Candyfloss, 15% choc ice in charge of a donkey! Mrs. Castle won't like this."

Scarborough

Daily Express, October 3, 1967

Yorkshire miners were considering going on an unofficial strike. In Wakefield, however, the wives told them, "No housework until you return to work" and told the press that they were refusing to buy food and were eating out for their meals.

"FLORRIE, we've got a blackleg at number 132."

The Local Government Boundary Commission was considering a few changes – not all were popular.

"Art thou trying to start another War of t'bloody Roses, Mr. Walker? Your new Yorkshire-Lancashire boundary goes right through my parlour."

Lancashire-Yorkshire border

Daily Express, February 18, 1971

Because of a rail strike in the Eastern and Southern regions, thousands of London commuters were having great difficulty getting to and from work in the City.

"You say you're running a Get-you-to-work service from South London to Westminster? Who's your navigator?"

At this time, British fisherman copied their French counterparts and blockaded a number of ports in protest against the importation of cut-price frozen fish.

"Captain Hornblower does it again – 'No traffic on the East Coast this time of the year, we'll hire a little boat and sail up as far as Grimsby...'"

Grimsby

Three months earlier, a strike by miners was terminated with an agreement to increase their pay after more than two days' intensive negotiations. Arthur Scargill, President of the Yorkshire branch of the National Union of Miners, had made it clear that he felt that much more for the miners could have been obtained from the agreement.

"I know as a miners' MP I've got to do everything Mr. Scargill tells me but I'm damn sure it doesn't include looking after your kids and doing your wife's shopping."

Sunday Express, June 29, 1975

Yorkshire

"Easy on the house-keeping, lass – we haven't got it yet."

Daily Express, July 8, 1975

An unfinished manuscript, by the wife of Hitler's half-brother, was published for the first time in 1979, which inferred that Hitler had stayed with them in Liverpool for a period during 1912.

"Dad, that story about Hitler living in Liverpool as a little boy – one Scouse teddy bear coming down."

96 Two days earlier the Education Secretary, Mark Carlisle, had been subject to a great deal of booing, hissing and jeering when giving a speech at a teachers' conference. The teachers were objecting to the Government's economic policies and more than 100 walked out of the meeting.

"If any of them shouted at me like they shouted at the Minister of Education I'd annihilate 'em."

Daily Express, April 10, 1980

"He found Skegness so bracing he's decided to come back to stay with his family."

"I can't bear people who address me as 'Luv' – especially when they follow it up with a crack across the head!"

Daily Express, April 10, 1984

"Oh, I don't know – for the last six Nationals, he's finished the course without me."

The South

"Now suppose we put it back where the Druids left it?"

Stonehenge

The strange desire of the British to paddle at least once a year.

Devon

"We're now going into Cornwall. So far, I believe Cornwall is in pretty good shape. Let's see if we can keep it that way."

Cornwall and Devon Lanes

Daily Express, August 22, 1951

"Dad'll get 'Fishermen of England' when he arrives home two hours late."

"Tea's ready, Don Juan!"

In the three days previous to this cartoon, truce talks in the Korean War broke down (not for the first time), and Britain, being at loggerheads with Persia (now Iran) over the oil situation, imposed a series of economic sanctions on the country.

"Sort of audience I like – half of 'em discussing Korea and the other half Persia."

A reference, perhaps, to Jonah and the fish.

"Mum! We've caught a lovely fish and Dad's still on the other end of the line."

No doubt Vera was dreaming of Gilbert and Sullivan's *The Pirates of Penzance*.

The dream of Vera...on a Penzance beach.

"Marvellous, isn't it? Come here every year for my holidays and go back every year telling 'em I've had a wonderful time."

Cornwall

Daily Express, August 29, 1951

"My family don't understand me – they want me to marry someone like Eve Perrick – but you – you're different."

"Vera and her love of Exmoor ponies – we'll arrive home like a bally rodeo."

The Labour government accused the Admiralty of trying to turn Dartmouth Naval College into a public school at taxpayer's expense with boys not from public schools having little chance of entering the college.

"Now tell me they don't favour Public Schoolboys at Dartmouth Naval College."

Rowers from the Soviet Union competed at the Henley Royal Regatta for the first time.

"Will it be all right if we clap if the Russians win?"

Henley

Daily Express, June 23, 1954

"Very good, Sergeant – replace bearskins."

The announcement that women may now study at Oxford in unlimited numbers was welcomed by most male undergrads. "But," said a well-known warden to a don, "kindly explain to little Miss Whatsit that such studies as boat-racing, the placing of utensils on spires, the debagging of Principals, were always – and shall remain – the undisputed privileges of the Male."

Oxford

Daily Express, February 1, 1957

"Dad! Dinner's served."

"Another refugee trying to escape to the West."

A report by the Advisory Centre of Education, in researching A-level results, stated the statistical revelation that, if there is any academic advantage to be gained by choice of school, it is in favour of the direct-grant and grammar schools rather than the independent public schools.

"Oh yeah, yeah, yeah?"

"When I said she's a bit wide across the beam I didn't mean you, you old faggot."

Cowes

At the Conservative Party conference at Brighton, it was suggested that the Party's image should be reviewed.

"I heard that, Martha – I heard that unfunny remark about my Tory Image could do with a bit of reshaping."

Daily Express, October 14, 1965

Brighton

This cartoon relates to an advertising campaign at the time.

"Bet they can't tell marge from butter."

Longleat Safari Park

"Horace! You're purring!"

Daily Express, May 26, 1966

Somerville College, Oxford

The 1967 FA Cup Final took place at Wembley three days before this cartoon appeared. It was the first final to be contested between two London teams, Tottenham Hotspur and Chelsea, and was thus dubbed the "Cockney Cup Final". Tottenham won 2–1. Presumably the ticket touts caught a cold.

"I don't care how much you lost touting tickets for the Cup Final – 'op it."

Plymouth

Daily Express, May 23, 1967

Sir Basil Smallpeice joined Cunard in April 1964, rising to chairman in November 1965, ultimately overseeing the QE2's project. **123**
Obviously the costs of the project were a worry.

"Phone Sir Basil and tell him first day's takings are good but thanks to souvenir hunters we now need a complete re-fit."

Daily Express, January 19, 1969   *Southampton*

A reference to Samuel Taylor Coleridge's sea-poem *The Rime of the Ancient Mariner*.

"Veronica, please don't emphasise your dislike of sailing by calling members of the Squadron 'Slimy things that crawl with legs upon a slimy sea'."

Cowes

Sunday Express, August 3, 1969

"Dumping them in the Solent and coming back for a new lot is not quite the idea, Commodore."

"Lady, you don't happen to have one about horses being unfair to riders?"

Badminton horse trials

Daily Express, April 30, 1974

New Zealander, Dame Naomi James, was the first woman to sail single-handedly around the world. She left Dartmouth, England in September 1977 and arrived back on June 8, 1978, after 272 days at sea.

"Darling, with your odd habit of always pulling the wrong ropes, promise me you'll never sail round a duck pond on your own."

128 This cartoon appeared two days after the birth of Zara Anne Elizabeth Phillips – the second child of Anne, Princess Royal and her first husband, Captain Mark Phillips.

"One can't start too early."

Gatcombe Park, Gloucestershire

Sunday Express, May 17, 1981

"Ahoy! Before you go – I want a word with one of you about my daughter!"

On July 21, 1981 the International Whaling Commission met at Brighton for their annual conference. On the agenda was a proposal for a worldwide ban on the commercial killing of whales but the failure to achieve the required three-fourths majority ensured that the ban did not pass.

"I'm afraid that whale the gentleman's been giving the kiss-of-life to for the last half hour happens to be one of these 'ere rubber ones."

Brighton

Daily Express, July 21, 1981

President Ronald Reagan, who frequently played a cowboy when a Hollywood star, had requested a bodyguard when he visited the Queen at Windsor Castle.

"Advance posse from the President – bodyguard to Two-gun Liz, Terror of Windsor Gulch."

"Simply riding your boy round Oxford on a tandem won't make him an Einstein, sir."

Oxford

Scotland

A Festival of Music and Drama has been held in Edinburgh every summer since 1947. There are now many additional events and concerts, which are known as the Edinburgh Fringe.

"Never heard Bach on the bagpipes before?"

"Mind your head, Michelangelo."

"Two miles from the Scottish border and first you tell me you don't drink Scotch and then you tell me you don't like haggis!!"

Daily Express, September 6, 1954

Scottish border

GILES in the heart of Scotland

"I ain't exactly a native, bud, but my grandpaw back in Texas was a buck sergeant under General Rabbie Burns right here in Perthshire."

Perthshire

"Well – we've seen Balmoral from the air, stalked our first deer... now what do we do?"

The Highland Games in 1954 coincided with the Farnborough Air Show, causing this dissent.

"I want to go to Farnborough Air Show!"

"Stand by for an acute attack of Grandma's deafness – I'm just going to tell her to get ready to go home."

The Highlands

"I see you're taking the Loch Ness Monster back with you."

Forth Bridge

Daily Express, September 18, 1954

Gretna Green is famous for runaway weddings, being the first village in Scotland on the old coaching route from London to Edinburgh. The local blacksmith and his anvil became the symbols of Gretna Green weddings.

"Married! Well, you just get straight back in there and get unmarried."

142 Eddie Calvert was an English trumpeter, who enjoyed great success in the 1950s. He had his first UK No. 1 in the Singles Chart in 1954, with his version of *Oh Mein Papa*, which was also in the US Top Ten.

"How does he do it? Signs himself 'Eddie Calvert,' that's how he does it."

"A pity Jock's wee missus came and fetched him in the middle of reciting 'A man's a man for a' that.'"

Sunday Express, January 25, 1959

Robbie Burns

"So much for our elopement making the headlines – telegram from your father thanking me very much."

Near Gretna Green

Two years earlier, US President "Ike" Eisenhower had hosted Elizabeth's first state visit to the US as Queen, and, in August 1959, "Ike" was a guest of the Queen at Balmoral. This cartoon relates to the preparation for the visit by the advance guard.

"Watch your step, Hank. Hostile native down there – fishing."

Ongoing surveillance for "Ike's" forthcoming visit.

President Ike's F.B.I. and our own Scotland Yard moving unobtrusively among the good people of Deeside making sure everything will be all right for the President's trip to Balmoral.

Deeside

Sounday Express, August 23, 1959

"If ye miss and hit one of yon bonnie submarines it'll be bang – goodnight Europe."

"And I say delivering your Scotch in time for Hogmanay or after is nae an essential service."

Throughout Scotland

Sunday Express, December 31, 1961

Pictures, taken by an American expedition, had been recently revealed appearing to show the Loch Ness Monster. Many people were convinced that they were authentic.

"I know they're in season but you'll be putting the wee bairns back – they're undersize."

"I think Nessie's the biggest con in the wurrld. Aye, but she's good for the tourist trade."

Loch Ness

Wales

At this time there was considerable debate about the need to preserve the Welsh language in education and elsewhere.

"Taffy, it don't make no sense ter me – why the 'eck ain't the Welsh wantin' ter speak Hinglish like the rest on us?"

Daily Express, February 19, 1953

Harlech Castle

The International Eisteddfod is held annually in Llangollen in July. Singing and dancing groups attend from all over the world, sharing their national folk traditions in one of the world's great festivals of the arts.

"To the stage, lads – and sorry I am if we do not bash the living daylights out of our opponents with 'Peace, perfect Peace'."

Llangollen

Sunday Express, July 12, 1953

Skiffle music was very popular, particularly amongst young people, at this time and was a mixture of jazz, blues, and folk, often using homemade or improvised instruments.

"The committee appreciates that skiffle has a place in an international festival, but we will not tolerate your referring to the rest of us as 'squares'."

154 The Sunday Closing (Wales) Act 1881 banned the sale of alcohol in Welsh pubs on the Sabbath. It was not repealed until 1961, when each county was charged with holding a referendum on Sunday opening to gauge support in their particular area.

"Here they come, Morgan. Don't forget – sorry we are to be so late, minister's sermon was twice as long this morning."

Merthyr

Sunday Express, November 12, 1961

"Rodney took some pretty silly bets in the bar last night about the strength of our future policies."

Daily Express, October 11, 1962

Llandudno

The investiture of Prince Charles as the twenty-first Prince of Wales took place at Caernarfon Castle on July 1, 1969.

"Call them off, Evans the Sheep, they'll want the Duke of Norfolk and Lord Snowdon back for dress rehearsal on Monday."

Caernarfon Castle

Sunday Express, June 29, 1969

"Nice one, Luv – get off the train and walk the rest of the way to Waterloo – you know the way."

The 1984 miners' strike was a major industrial action affecting the British coal industry.

"It's not official yet – just a practice run."

This refers either to the Local Authority elections or the UK European Parliament elections which were held in June 1984.

"She let us give her a lift to her polling booth providing we dropped her off at her sister's on the way home."

Sunday Express, May 6, 1984

Mid Wales

British Cartoon Archive

The cartoons here were taken from originals in Carl Giles's private archive, a huge collection of artwork, ephemera and correspondence, and in the British Cartoon Archive at the University of Kent, much of this fascinating collection can be seen online at www.cartoons.ac.uk

Giles's papers show that he didn't really enjoy foreign holidays. "I went to the South of France once,"

Giles at work in his caravan

he told an interviewer, but found only "last year's Lucky Strike cigarette packets flip-flapping about in the tideless Mediterranean, obsequious waiters and nothing to do". As a cartoonist and social observer he preferred touring Britain, noting that "a wander around keeps the ideas coming".

To help this creative process Giles built himself a studio caravan. "I tour the country a good deal," he explained, but "never get the right facilities for drawing in a boarding house or hotel". Construction began in November 1950, using "one rough drawing as a guide and a local boy as assistant". It was finished in six months, and included an easel under the sloping windows and a bar with a rail "just the right height for standing" which conveniently folded down into a double bed.

In May 1951 Giles took the caravan on its first tour, but sadly he had miscalculated the weight, and one of the wheels promptly gave way. He located and fitted two heavy-duty lorry wheels, and carried on, but after a couple of seasons decided on a complete rebuild. The new vehicle took to the road in August 1954, with several refinements, including a telephone and teleprinter to keep in touch with the *Express*. But the crowning glory was a studio extension that folded out from the side, with two large windows to catch the light.

According to Giles the new caravan was so well-equipped "that it's not like going away at all". Express Newspapers agreed to give him an extra £250 a year (£6,000 in today's money) "to meet the abnormal expenses you incur in making your caravan tours", plus an expense account that funded lavish entertaining. Lord Beaverbrook described the caravan as "a mobile off-licence", and, according to one *Express* journalist, whenever it stopped, "the door flew wide, the bar flew open, [and] the studio was lowered with the gentle hiss of well-oiled machinery", leaving Giles ready to start business.

The famous customized caravan